Literary Houses

For Mary Ansdell
with love

Literary Houses

Rosalind Ashe

Paper Tiger

A Dragon's World Ltd. Imprint

Dragon's World Ltd.,
Limpsfield,
Surrey RH8 ODY
Great Britain

Design and Art Direction by Steve Henderson
Plans sketched by David Heal

Hardback: ISBN 0 905895 61 4
Limpback: ISBN 0 905895 64 9

Printed in Hong Kong

FOREWORD

A house is a box, with a lid, and something moving inside it. So is a book; and this is a book about houses, boxes within boxes.

Imagine *Rebecca* without Manderley or Count Dracula without his castle; put the powerful and sinister Jay Gatsby into a service flat, or Mr Rochester into a thatched cottage—and you will see that the houses in these novels are more than mere stage sets: they are almost 'characters'. They linger in your mind long after the book is closed. They have become real.

But why do mere bricks, stones and mortar—real or fictional—have this power over our imaginations? It may be to do with their continuity, spanning many human lives; and it is hard for even the most down-to-earth of us to resist the strong impression that, in some strange, organic way, those old walls actually store impressions of the generations they have sheltered. What tales these walls could tell… Fictional houses share the reverberative quality—but in fiction, those tales are told.

We have taken ten well-known novels set in the past, and explored the houses in them. Some of these houses watch things happen; others make things happen; and in all there is an element of mystery, whether it is the granite bastion of Baskerville Hall, over which there hangs a deadly curse, Dorian Gray's elegant Mayfair residence with its locked attic, or Miss Havisham's living tomb.

Knowing that everyone's ideas will be different—a picture built from fragments of houses half-seen, of childhood homes, movie images—we realise ours is only a possibility. All we have, in the end, is the book itself, and to that in each case we have been faithful. When we follow Maxim de Winter's nervous new wife along the corridors of Manderley, or retrace Jonathan Marker's steps through Castle Dracula, we have stuck with the text like time-travelling sleuths. And only the text: that is, we have not visited the various existing sources—Menabilly in Cornwall, the Turner House in Salem—deliberately using the atmosphere, scattered hints and flavour of the book itself as departure point on our voyage of discovery. Brief biographies supply the facts about the authors, and the buildings they may have drawn on; what we take is only what they have chosen to give us, and it is this we explore.

So this is a book by a reader for readers, not by a scholar for pupils: our aim is to entertain—to intrigue the newcomer, to stimulate the connoisseur, into reading or re-reading these classics.

Ten old houses, ten mysteries, in pictures and words. Turn the page, and you open a door.

CONTENTS

CONTENTS

Daphne du Maurier
1907-

Daphne du Maurier was born and spent her early years in London. She was educated at home and at a Paris finishing school. She started writing in 1928 and, with the publication of *Rebecca* in 1938, she established herself as a highly successful author. Her popularity was enhanced by Alfred Hitchcock's films of *Rebecca* and *My Cousin Rachel* (1951). The famous house of *Rebecca*, Manderley, is Daphne du Maurier's tribute to "Menabilly", her home near Fowey in Cornwall, where she lived between 1943 and 1967.

Daphne du Maurier married in 1932. Her late husband, Lt. Gen. Sir Frederick 'Boy' Browning was Treasurer to the Duke of Edinburgh.

Chapter 1

REBECCA

'We turned the last corner, and so came to Manderley. Yes, there it was, the Manderley I had expected, the Manderley of my picture post-card long ago. A thing of grace and beauty, exquisite and faultless, lovelier even than I had ever dreamed, built in its hollow of smooth grassland and mossy lawns, the terraces sloping to the gardens, and the gardens to the sea.'

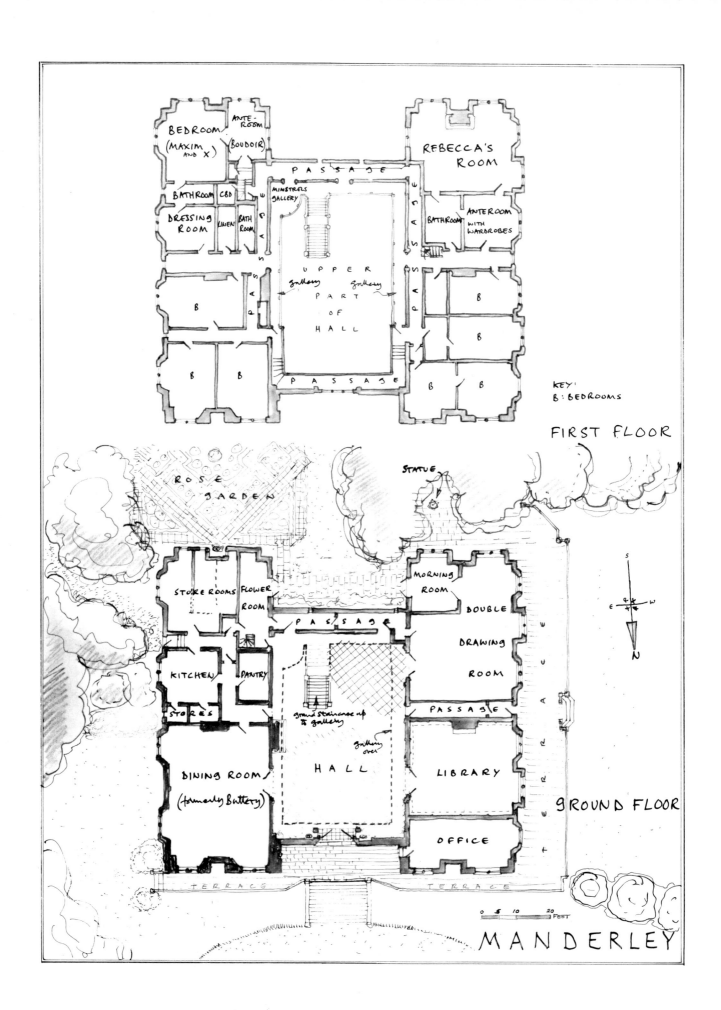

BEDROOM (MAXIM AND X) ANTE-ROOM BOUDOIR

REBECCA'S ROOM

BATHROOM CBD MINSTRELS GALLERY PASSAGE

DRESSING ROOM LINEN BATH ROOM

BATHROOM ANTEROOM WITH WARDROBES

UPPER PART OF HALL

Gallery Gallery

B B B B

PASSAGE B B

KEY: B : BEDROOMS

FIRST FLOOR

ROSE GARDEN

STATUE

STORE ROOMS FLOWER ROOM

MORNING ROOM

DOUBLE DRAWING ROOM

PASSAGE

KITCHEN PANTRY

STORES

PASSAGE

ground staircase up to gallery

gallery over

HALL

LIBRARY

GROUND FLOOR

DINING ROOM (formerly Buttery)

OFFICE

S E W N

TERRACE TERRACE

0 5 10 20 FEET

MANDERLEY

THE notice on the high iron gates said 'Open to the public every Wednesday'; and it was Friday. The postcard I had bought in the village shop was a distant view, hand-tinted and framed with blood-red rhododendrons; it was the house itself that had held my eye, caught my imagination. I was determined to see it before I left Cornwall; so I set off through the woods, making a wide circle, until I came out on a low cliff. The air was still. In the mild afternoon light a silver sea crumbled to creamy foam on the teeth of a rocky inlet. Above it, set among smooth green lawns and enfolding woods, stood Manderley: mellow, serene, and so very private—almost secret—it drew me on.

Skirting the rhododendron thicket that bordered the lower lawn, I drew nearer; now I could see the warm cut stone softened by lichen and the salt winds of three hundred years. There was no one in the grounds, no movement at the open windows; and the first floor casements towards the sea were blank and shuttered. At this corner the ground fell away steeply to the rocks below; and I wondered what it would be like in winter and rough weather, and how you would listen to the crashing of the waves—how the mists would stream across, hiding the headland and the secret, beautiful house...

All at once there was a noise of barking; two cocker spaniels scampered out of the trees and across the lawn, then a young woman following them. She was in her early twenties, perhaps, but more like a schoolgirl: awkward and shy as she halted then came toward me. Plain skirt, straight hair, no make-up.

I apologised for trespassing. 'It was this postcard,' I said. She took it, smiling, and suddenly pretty. 'Really? That's how I first saw it too... I say, no one's around—Mrs Danvers has gone to Lanyon. Just a quick look—we'd only be a moment.' 'I'd love to,' I said. 'The hall is quite famous, isn't it?' 'The show-piece. Yes.'

She led me round by the gravel drive, up the steps and into the huge cool hall, two stories high. 'There you are: minstrels' gallery and all.' Her voice had dropped to a whisper, and as I gazed round at the pannelled walls, the ranks of portraits, the carved oak staircase leading up to the gallery, I found myself whispering too, treading softly as she did on the echoing stone paving—and wondering where *she* fitted in this house, 'family seat of the de Winters for many centuries' as the postcard told me: a secretary perhaps? A housekeeper? No, too young and too uncertain for that—

'They have a great ball here every summer,' she was saying. 'Or they used to. People are always talking about it...' Her voice trailed away; then: 'The portraits, now. That's a Lely; a Gainsborough, a Van Dyke over there, that huge one.' I asked her about the girl in white at the top of the staircase. 'That's by Raeburn. It's of Catherine de Winter. She was a famous beauty in her time, you know. That's before she was married. She's lovely, isn't she?... All these doors! I got quite lost my first day. The dining room, the way to the kitchens, then the flower-room. That's the drawing room: another show-piece. But the nicest room is really this one, the library. Have a look. This is—well, Mr de Winter's favourite, I think. A bit untidy—newspapers and things—but I love it.'

It was certainly a handsome room, very casual, very unself-conscious, very masculine. (And she's got a bit of a crush on the

I found my eyes returning to the portrait of the girl in white at the head of the staircase. Her sidelong glance was curiously seductive, and though clearly young, she looked wilful—dangerous perhaps. Almost wanton.

master of the house, I thought.) The great drawing room next door was in complete contrast; here all was formal and fragile, the hand-picked ornaments—Dresden figures, cool green Chinese pots—arranged consciously on the thoroughbred furniture. This panelling had been painted French grey, and the pictures (I recognised a Canaletto, a small Watteau) seemed chosen for the blue damask up-holstery, just as the great alabaster vase of mauve lilac echoed the pastel silk curtains. 'Perfect, isn't it?' she said. 'Only Mrs Danvers dusts in here.' (*And* she's scared of this Mrs Danvers, I thought.) 'Very impressive,' I said, hunting for words to cover the chill this

Right: '*The hall is really famous: the show-piece,' she said. 'They have a great ball here every summer—or used to.*'

20

'The library', she said. 'Not a show-room. But isn't it—sympathetic? So much more lived in. The dogs love it too... And tea is served in here...'

room gave me. But she was leading me through to a smaller one beyond. 'This is the morning room. That's Mrs de Winter's desk.'

Another exquisite apartment, dominated by the bowls of scarlet rhododendrons, and more outside framing the statue of a white marble faun. The desk was the focal point, open to show neat ranks of thick creamy stationary, labelled compartments—'household', 'social', 'financial'—two telephones, diary, menu book: all defined by the same flowing handwriting—large, confident and black. This was the seat of power, then. Here the Canaletto—or the salmon mousse—is ordered, I thought; the summer ball organized—the strong black pen making or breaking as it ticks or crosses the social list... I felt admiration for this Mrs Maxim de Winter, but I did not like her.

'A powerful lady,' I said, longing to say more, to ask— 'One more room,' she said. 'Here, this way.' Swiftly, almost furtively, she led me through passages, up stairs and along another passage. Now I could hear the sea closer and louder.

The room we entered was large and nearly dark, with all the mystery and latent drama of an unlit stage. She switched on a lamp then opened one pair of shutters. 'This is her bedroom,' she said; 'I suppose it's the most beautiful room in the house.' I gazed round the room with its wide casements, the carved fireplace running full height, and the ornate plasterwork of the ceiling. There were rich hangings and old tapestry chairs, doors half-open on closets full of glimmering gowns. A silken wrap hung over a chair; the nightdress

The morning room was exquisite, the same flawless taste in china, in pictures, in colour—dominated by the bowls of scarlet rhododendrons, and by the personality of Rebecca.

23

was laid out ready across the quilt of the huge bed. Whether it was the perfume bottles on the dressing table or the bowls of red rhododendrons or the seductive fragrance of Mrs de Winter herself, the whole room seemed to breathe it, and I felt the presence of someone vibrant, and alive: if I leaned down and touched those slippers, they would be still warm.

I found a fisherman's hut and boathouse in the next cove; there was a dinghy drawn up. Months later I saw the significance of its painted name, Je Reviens.

Hastily, as though sharing my unease, the girl closed the shutters and led me back the way we had come. 'The servants will be about, preparing tea,' she said over her shoulder. 'Better slip out quickly—here. Go down by the cove—' I had so much to ask; already she was turning away. I said, 'Thank you. But suppose we'd been caught. Wouldn't Mrs de Winter have been angry?' She looked startled. 'But didn't you know? Mrs de Winter—Rebecca—is dead: those rooms are kept shut like that, always.' She was gone.

Sounds from the servants' wing. I cut across the lawn towards the sea, ran down a steep path between banks of azaleas, out onto the shore and over a rocky headland. In the next cove was an old dinghy, and a fisherman's hut; but I could hear a distant car, and the dogs barking. No time for exploration; I felt I had already seen too much. I trekked up through the woods back to the road.

Two things only I learned from local talk; Rebecca had been drowned sailing; and Maxim de Winter had married again—very different the new one was. But two months later it was all over the front pages: 'Coroner's Inquest Reopened', 'Suspicion of Murder', and the final haunting photographs of Manderly in ruins.

Charles Dickens
1812-1870

Charles Dickens was born in Portsea, near Portsmouth. He was brought up in poverty—much of it in London—and his father was imprisoned for debt in the Marshalsea. Dickens never forgot the degradation of poverty; it informed all his writings and crusades for social reform. He worked as a reporter for the *Morning Chronicle,* but the success of his first novel, *The Pickwick Papers* (1836-7), allowed him to devote all his energies to writing and campaigning. Dickens enthusiastically supported a number of causes, ranging from international copyright to the abolition of slavery. In 1850, he started a periodical called *Household Words,* to which he contributed, often in collaboration with Wilkie Collins, several short stories. *Great Expectations* was first published, during 1860-61, in his second periodical, *All the Year Round.* It is likely that Miss Havisham's 'Satis House' was modelled on a house known simply as "Restoration House" in The Vines area of Rochester, Kent, where Dickens lived. In his later years, Dickens' many visits abroad—to America, Italy and Switzerland—were often accompanied by public readings from his works. The energy of his performances is thought to have contributed to his early death at the age of fifty-eight.

Chapter 2

GREAT EXPECTATIONS

'I had stopped to look at the house as I passed; and its seared red brick walls, blocked windows, and strong green ivy clasping even the stacks of the chimneys with its twigs and tendons, as if with sinewy old arms, had made up a rich attractive mystery, of which I was the hero.'

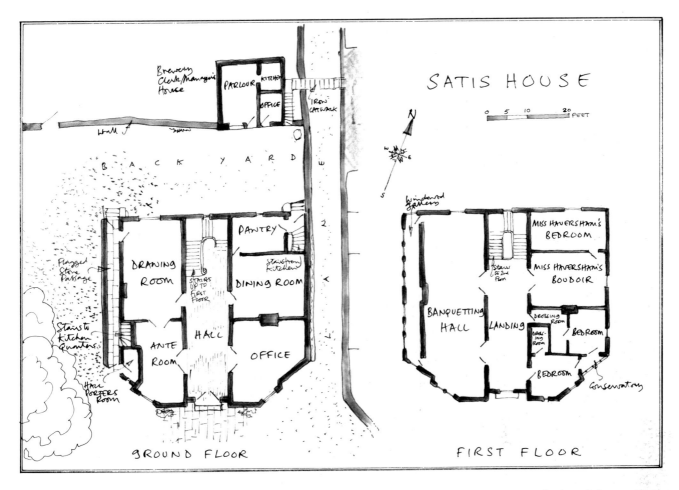

SATIS HOUSE

0 5 10   20 FEET

GROUND FLOOR

FIRST FLOOR

Satis house was a superior dwelling on the outskirts of the town, backed by a large walled garden; beyond lay salt flats and the Medway estuary. It must have been very grand indeed when old Mr Havisham built it in the 1760s beside the brewery that he ran—more as a hobby, you understand: fine gentlemen do not touch trade.

A high wall protected Satis House from the street; through the iron gates passers-by could see the front court and fine entrance and, separated by an alleyway, the main body of the malt-house with its tall chimney behind. Now tall grasses grew between the paving stones; two stout chains guarded the front door, and the disused brewery was open to the sky. The great house itself stood blind and shuttered; engulfing ivy had reached right up to the chimneys.

But it was not deserted. Thin smoke rose from one chimney. Someone was still living there. Stranger still, she was rich and—in her way—powerful. The only daughter of the gentleman brewer, she too had a hobby, an absorbing pastime: Miss Havisham devoted thirty years of self-imposed seclusion to revenge.

Visitors—and there were few apart from her lawyer and her inheritance-hungry relatives—had to ring a bell by the gate; admitted after some delay, they were taken into the house through a side door. Inside all was dark and shuttered; by candlelight they were led along a stone passage across another courtyard to a pokey parlour, and waited for her summons. When it came they trooped back into the great house and up the shuttered staircase. On the landing, a solitary wheelchair, and beyond it the wide, handsome corridor. A

Visitors were admitted by a side door, led along a stone passage and out again across another courtyard to wait in the small house where the brewery manager must have lived. Here, in a pokey parlour looking out on the ruined kitchen garden, the women conversed guardedly about Miss Havisham's health, while the menfolk paced and waited for her summons.

31

light shone under one of the closed doors. Inside was a strange room lit by fire and candlelight.

It was the boudoir of a grand lady, spacious and well furnished, but in some disarray: trunks standing open, fine gowns, bonnets, shawls and laces lying about in all the glamorous confusion of an imminent journey. But there was no movement, except the flickering of the coals. Even the candle flames stood straight in the heavy, motionless air; no sound came from the clock on the mantle shelf: its hands had stopped at twenty minutes to nine. Indeed, the whole room was like a picture of arrested activity, a faded sepia print. The tight bouquet of flowers was the same: unopened brown buds, and the skeletal frames of long-dead fern. That satin shoe had never touched the ground: a museum piece now, like all the finery round it.

Miss Havisham was not nearly as old as gossip would have it: still in her forties—but as frail and withered as the rosebuds by her looking glass. Sitting there in veiled, bejewelled and threadbare grandeur, she held her parchment hands out to the fire, and watched the youth playing at cards with Estella, her beautiful young ward; being beaten and coming back for more. Watched him falling in love. She barely acknowledged her visiting cousins standing inside the door. Estella ignored them. They were accustomed to that; but they looked hard at the lad: they had seen him there before, and were beginning to suspect some scheme of the old girl's—might she actually adopt him? Marry him to Estella, and leave them all her money? Miss Havisham was eccentric, but not mad: that was the

Branching candlesticks lit a dressing table cluttered with flowers, gloves, prayer book—even a white satin shoe.

Right: *Those fashionable gowns and bonnets were a generation out of date: all the whites—and white predominated—were crisp and yellow as parchment.*

trouble. A mind unhinged might have been easier to plan round, even to pity; it was her singlemindedness that puzzled them and made them watchful. Odd, the way her private tragedy had taken her—not a real tragedy of course: the man had been a rascal when all was said and done, and she should be grateful she was spared. But what was she up to now, sitting there watching the two young people, like some Persian cat, all bright eyes and starting white hair?

Miss Havisham knew just what she was up to. She had reared her bait, chosen her victim; one day she would watch her lovely Estella play out the drama planned so long, alone in that silent house, her chosen tomb.

She had been twenty-six when it happened: not beautiful, but very rich, and savouring her reign as a courted, pampered heiress. Then she fell in love; and her life became a whirl of preparation, of Paris gowns and Irish linens, of wedding lists and presents—especially those extravagant keepsakes she showered on her love. A time of delicious anticipation, of great expectations. On the morning of her wedding day at twenty minutes to nine, a message arrived from her fiancé that he was not going through with the marriage. At that moment her heart broke. She stopped everything. Nothing was to change from that moment on: her boudoir, her house, her life would be a memorial to her murdered heart. At twenty minutes to nine that fateful morning she had one shoe on: she would wear one shoe for ever.

Now her stockinged foot was bare; her elaborately coiffed hair had grown into a wild white bird's nest, her wedding dress had frayed to tatters waiting for the bridegroom. But her eyes watched Estella, in the finest of her jewels, ensnaring the boy who would soon be a man, and whose heart would be broken in payment...

Now Miss Havisham was ready for her excursion—let the poor relations wait and mutter among themselves! She summoned Pip and leant on his arm—how tall he had grown! He helped her into the wicker wheelchair and pushed her down the corridor to the door of the banqueting chamber. This was the finest room in the house. Miss Havisham could remember when it had been filled with sunlight and movement, and especially on that morning... Latterly she found it suited her mood, and made a change from the dry faded boudoir. Today a weak fire struggled in the grate—it was rarely lit—and a mist of chill smoke hung in the air. Heavy curtains covered the shuttered windows so that no chink of light could come through—but the spiders and vermin had found a way; and in such dank darkness the very walls were alive with creeping mould. Now the tall candles revealed a grotesque indoor jungle, clinging garlands of cobwebs, pale fungus, the half-seen twitch of spiders; in the silence, only the susurrus of mice, the creak of the wheelchair.

For now it was all she wanted. 'Satis' means: enough.

Right: The ruined malt-house, with its wilderness of casks, was a fine playground to escape into after Miss Havisham's stuffy shuttered rooms.

Right overleaf: She could remember that brilliant morning, with the servants laying the long table for the wedding breakfast, when the great tiered cake had been carried in and set in the centre... It was a long time before she had ventured in there again to brood over the ruined feast.

40

Even to the inveterately curious, entrance halls and anterooms give little away; but we were immediately struck by the dual impression of luxury and a curious asceticism.

THE 'Sale of Contents' notice on the door of a certain house in Grosvenor Square was so discreet as to raise the immediate suspicion it was aimed only at those in the trade or in the know. Such deliberate privacy over a public announcement is irresistible: we rang the bell. A whiskered gentleman filling the half-open door demanded to know if we were 'genuine purchasers'; whether our Intentions were Serious. Assuring him that intention is always serious—only action is frivolous—we bluffed our way into the hall.

This was elegant but austere in line after all the draped mantles, petticoated furniture and elaborate overcrowding of the High Victorian houses we knew from an exhausting social round—and furnished with two tantalizing extremes of taste: a luscious 18th century French clock and a simple Greek Narcissus, cast in silver. Through open doors we could see a large library where half a dozen men of the trade were turning over vases, pulling out drawers and fingering curtains. It was a double room, bow-ended onto the garden; in the antechamber the new taste for things Japanese had been effectively indulged, while the main library—clearly the haunt of literati rather than of fustian scholars—reinforced the original impression of mingled sensuality and eclecticism: plain blue-grey walls, cream blinds, cold marble busts and a breakfast table in the window of monkish simplicity. But the blinds were finest silk; the table spread, it seemed, with some rich altar cloth; and the Chinese rose bowl, the looking glass wreathed in cupids, the richly cushioned sofa, the looped partition curtain, glimmering somewhere between grape and *marron*—all were chosen, one sensed, very consciously, and by that rare bird, a passionate aesthete. Who was he? Did he die? Or merely change his tastes and move on?

Two dealers were talking in the next room. 'A very rum do altogether,' said one. 'Family wanted it hushed up, that's certain,' said his companion; 'not that there's much family as such—and the so-called friends just popped in, took a couple of priceless momentos, I hear, and vanished away.' 'Didn't want any scandal to rub off on 'em—right? And as for that; marvellous—eh?—how little of it got into the papers.' 'Pals in high places, mark my words—' 'But not too many at the funeral, I hear...'

We moved on into the room where the speakers stood leafing through some drawings on an easel, and they fell silent. This, we found, was the bedroom, an unusual octagonal chamber looking south into the garden; it had apparently been created from a large bell-shaped room, a noble, single-storey pavilion, by panelling off the corners that flanked the fireplace—and these had become wardrobes, and a valet's entrance from the back hall, masked by concealed doors. The silk-covered panels carried on round the bow, completing the false octagon with a triple arched window; and into this had been set a fanciful bed, looped and garlanded with layers of fine drapery through which the sun shimmered, catching on a multitude of glinting threads, and doubly gilding the attendant putti. Standing by the bed-head, one could see that the room had been designed and decorated from here: the Tang horse, the kneeling wooden angel looted from some Spanish church, the lofty shelf of exotic stringed instruments, the nude black marble statue decked out with mitre, crozier, and embroidered alb—all faced towards,

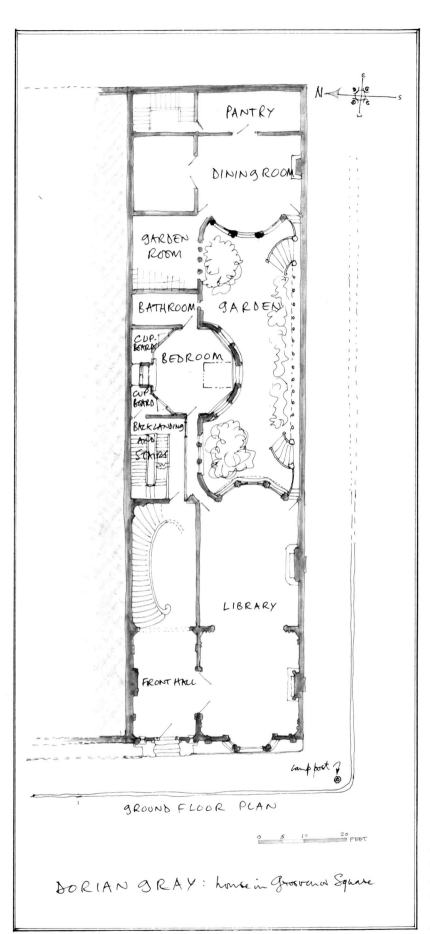

PANTRY

DINING ROOM

GARDEN ROOM

BATHROOM

GARDEN

CUP-BOARD

BEDROOM

CUP-BOARD

BACK LANDING AND STAIRS

LIBRARY

FRONT HALL

lamp post

GROUND FLOOR PLAN

0 5 10 20 FEET

DORIAN GRAY: house in Grosvenor Square

It had been his grandfather's, we were told, a stern forbidding guardian under whose rule he had been reared. As soon as the Mayfair house was his, with the wealth to make it truly his, he landscaped the gardens, turned two ground floor pavilions into his bedroom and his dining hall, banished all the heavy dark furniture to the country estate and filled his bachelor home with comfort and beauty. Only the schoolroom in the attic remained unchanged.

acknowledged, their absent master's high-piled satin pillows. The fireplace was surrounded by a pretty French mantel of maroon marble with lapis slips, and above it there hung a fine Waterford looking-glass, angled downward onto those pillows. On either side was a pair of well-preserved Renaissance tapestries: votive processions winding through Tuscan landscapes, where lords and warriors were followed by a train of pretty pages, dwarfs, and fantastic creatures.

Even the hardened dealers about us seemed momentarily awed by this array. 'Some nice pieces' was the cautious consensus. 'A famous collector of course,' pronounced one solemnly, breaking ranks to examine the angel for woodworm (its supplicant hands, I now saw, held a sprinkling of visiting cards). 'But you'll find none of your popular type of item here—eh, Mr Spink? A collector's collector, as one might say.' 'Very true,' replied the august personage so addressed. Sage nods all round, and a moment of silence. 'But one that knew all about comfort,' he added, throwing open the door to an inner bathroom.

The floor was paved in onyx, the walls lined with Turkish tiles, and the fittings were mahogany and brass—the bath itself a veritable pavilion, a brass birdcage of curtain-rails and pierced pipes arranged to spray the occupant from every angle. With a tall white marble statue of Pomona, a deep, fur rug, a lacquered cane bookcase and table, a large easy chair and a soft, suede-covered footstool, this bathroom lacked nothing but austerity; and yet, set in this era of ours, it amounted to a selection that could not be accused of excess.

'The taps and so forth,' said Mr Spink, 'as I have ascertained and verified, are clever imitations: yes, gentlemen, they have all been expertly tinted to look like brass, but are, in fact, gold. Nine carat, but gold.' 'I wonder if he bit it,' said my companion as we made our way back to the library.

We were examining the books, including some rare French works—and a few privately bound volumes for very specialised tastes.

'Not of the family, are you, my dear sirs?' It was the whiskered gentleman. 'Nor the trade, I feel certain. What is your field precisely, sir?'—addressing me direct. 'We are pickers up of considered trifles, my good man,' I replied: 'yes, private collectors if you wish; and Americans, as you may have judged for yourself, visiting friends and salerooms on the way to the Continent. Tell us, who was this Mr'—I consulted the ornate Ex Libris on the flyleaf of the book I held—'this Mr Dorian Gray? And why this somewhat hugger-mugger disposal of his worldly goods?'

'Mr Gray was a wealthy man-about-town, sir; and he died suddenly some fortnight ago, under circumstances peculiar, rather than downright suspicious: the verdict was suicide. But there were—how shall I put it?—certain scandals attached to his name that persuaded the interested parties to dispose quietly of his collections, preferring to realize a small inheritance as a discreet cheque than face the publicity attendant on, say, a sale at Christie's... Not to mention,' he added, 'the more esoteric collectors' items that have already been removed.'

Now we were on the second floor; we had been shown the other receptions rooms and bedrooms, some of which housed the

exotic jewelry collection, the racks of High Church vestments, the tallboys packed with silks, damasks and brocades, and glass cases full of a strange array of musical instruments, from sitars to nose-flutes. 'But the most remarkable item, I consider,' said our guide, 'is on the top floor: of no value, it seems, to the trade—though bids have been put in for the Italian *cassone* in the same lot—Up here, in the old schoolroom. A very fine portait of Mr Gray.'

Surprisingly elaborate grilles and locks had once barred the door of this large attic, as though to preserve some secret. Now we entered freely, but stopped short: the room was a shock after all the preceding taste and elegance. It was low and sombre, with heavy furniture and hangings all covered in grime, dust and cobwebs. Only two patches of colour there were: the dried blood on the floor where the drugget tacked across it had been trodden back, and the blazing beauty of the portait.

'There you are, sirs: that's him to the life—I saw him in a sale-room not a week before his demise.' 'Was he so *young*?' I asked, loud in the sudden silence. 'But this house contains the collection of a lifetime!' 'That was the extraordinary thing, sir—and why, in my humble opinion the whole thing was hushed up. It wasn't just the scandals—the drugs, the low-life, his strange pastimes or even the rumour that Mr Gray was the direct cause of two tragic suicides. It was the problem they had identifying the body: they only knew him by his rings. The dead man was twice as old as Mr Gray, they said—and hideously ugly.'

His collections included jewelry, vestments, rare books, exotic musical instruments, rich fabrics, statues, paintings; but through all ran this fascination with the trappings of religion.

His octagonal bedchamber had been created in a large bell-shaped room with triple windows onto the garden.

This schoolroom was heavy with memories of his lonely childhood, and his innocence—better locked away and forgotten; and returned to only to hide, and to visit, his terrible secret.

49

Nathaniel Hawthorne
1804-1864

Nathaniel Hawthorne was born in Salem, Massachusetts. He was a descendant of Major William Hawthorne, one of the first Puritan settlers in America. He was educated at Bowdouin College, Brunswick, Maine, but decided to continue his studies no further. Instead, he entered the Customs Office in Salem in 1846 as a Surveyor. In 1853, he was sent as American Consul to Liverpool, England. Hawthorne's attachment to Salem, however, is manifest in the painstaking attention to details of town life in *The House of the Seven Gables* (1853).

Chapter 4

THE HOUSE OF
THE SEVEN GABLES

' "Now see;—under those seven gables, at which we now look up—and which old Colonel Pyncheon meant to be the house of his descendants, in prosperity and happiness, down to an epoch far beyond the present—under that roof, through a portion of three centuries, there has been perpetual remorse of conscience, a constantly defeated hope, strife amongst kindred, various misery, a strange form of death, dark suspicion, unspeakable disgrace." '

I WRITE this account as some sort of farewell to the strange old house wherein I have lodged these past months. Such dramas and reversals of fortune have befallen its occupants of late, and so gladly do we now take our leave of it, that this backward glance may appear sentimental, even morbid; but a house that has, through a century and a half, been the chief source of local speculation and legend surely deserves at least an obituary.

It was built in 1690 or thereabouts by Colonel Pyncheon, on two acres of land acquired, it was said, by means which at best were within the letter of the law but which certainly boded no good. Matthew Maule, who for forty years since its first settlement, had cleared and worked the land, was arraigned and executed for the crime of witchcraft; whereupon the rich and powerful Colonel, having for some time sought to possess the plot, swiftly achieved his goal. Where Maule's humble shack had stood, he built the mighty Pyncheon House, or the House of the Seven Gables, as it came to be known.

Now, legend has it that, with his dying breath, Matthew Maule

Right: *The Colonel's mansion now stood where Matthew Maule's humble shack had been; and many wondered at his building his home over that of the dead wizard, giving the ghost a kind of freedom to haunt the grand new rooms.*

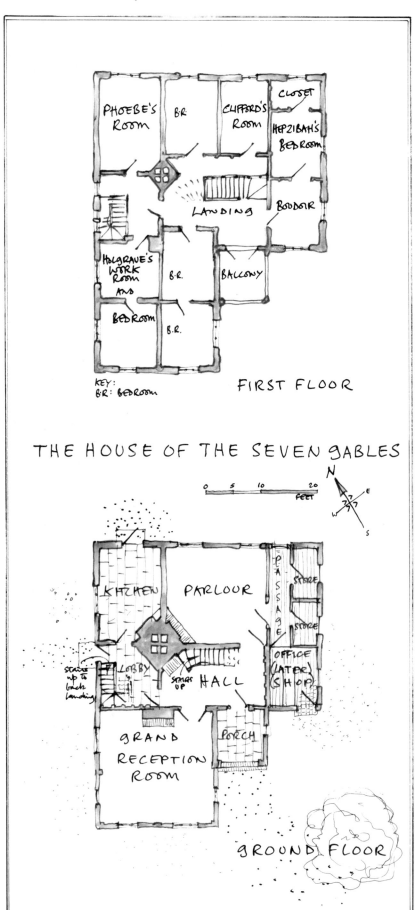

PHOEBE'S ROOM

B.R.

CLIFFORD'S ROOM

CLOSET

HEPZIBAH'S BEDROOM

LANDING

BOUDOIR

HOLGRAVE'S WORK ROOM AND BEDROOM

B.R.

BALCONY

B.R.

KEY:
B.R: BEDROOM

FIRST FLOOR

THE HOUSE OF THE SEVEN GABLES

0   5   10   20
            FEET

N
E
W
S

KITCHEN

PARLOUR

PASSAGE

STORE

STORE

OFFICE (LATER) SHOP

Stairs up to back Landing

LOBBY

STAIRS UP

HALL

GRAND RECEPTION ROOM

PORCH

GROUND FLOOR

The ground plan was based on that of the basic timber cabin, but aggrandised beyond recognition to three storeys and no less than seven gables.

Right: *In earlier days the Pyncheons had fallen on hard times; an ancestor of Miss Hepzibah's had installed a shop in the corner of the house adjoining the street. Now she found herself so hard-pressed she was reduced to opening it. She swept and dusted it, stocked it with supplies and nervously awaited the first customer.*

The room where Phoebe was put to sleep was gaunt and forbidding. Even the tall dark chair seemed to sit and watch beside her through the night.

(with no change of expression) her wretched nervousness and irresolution on that dark day when poverty drove her to open the shop: a Pyncheon reduced to Trade!

But that was also the day young Phoebe came into her life—and mine. A country cousin of old Hepzibah's, she arrived on the doorstep without warning, bringing sunshine and hope to the old house. And it *was* old by then: nearly a hundred and sixty years since its bright new pargetting had dazzled all eyes. Now only crumbs of that plaster remained, and the oak frame had been blackened by wind and weather. Weeds sprouted from the shingles, and the two-acre plot had dwindled to a neglected garden bounded by poor back streets of the spreading, thriving town.

The garden, at least, I had attempted to improve in my spare hours. I succeeded in producing some fine vegetables; but it required Phoebe's encouragement and industry to tame the flower beds and lawn, to restore the rickety summer-house and make the prospect so pleasing that even old Hepzibah came out from under her dark gables to sit there. It became the favourite haunt of her brother Clifford, a sad, faded man whose prime had been wasted within prison walls. Phoebe and her garden were all his delight; and, like the scrawny cock and hens she fed each day, he flourished in her care.

So it was that four of us were dwelling in the Pyncheon House through that final summer, the summer which opened with Phoebe's knock at the door, and now closes on a dark, empty mansion. But in

In her boudoir with its faded curtains and quaint old furniture, Hepzibah kept her most beloved possession, hidden away inside the draw of her desk. It was a miniature of a beautiful young man.

'Ok so you've only three days in New York, but you've got to go to a party at Gatsby's,' they said. Some of them had met him, no-one seemed to know what he did, but his parties were *de rigueur*: all the best people went, and lots of others as well, often uninvited: you'd always find someone there you knew who would know someone who knew Gatsby.

Twenty miles due east of New York and jutting out into Long Island Sound are the peninsulas of East Egg and West Egg. Both, I gathered, were expensively residential; but there was a subtle difference in the sort of money that resided in upmarket, high-society East Egg and the slightly shady millions just across the bay. This was '22, '23, remember: the early days of the jazz era and prohibition, when any rich man well known for throwing wild parties, and regularly, was at once desirable and suspect.

Well, Gatsby lived on West Egg. A few years back he had bought this mansion from some big brewer, who built it in about 1908, during the 'period' craze. Modelled full-size on a Normandy Hotel de Ville, it stood in forty acres complete with terraces, gardens, mooring, stables and marble pool: the instant Ancestral Home. As we approached it through its postern entrance, we could see the feudal silhouette against the evening light.

Already the long drive and the wide gravel sweep were thronged with cars; bright young things grouped themselves decoratively on steps and along the balustrade, or flitted through the wide verandah. The music came sweet and loud from a band on the terrace, while the duck-egg sky darkened behind a blaze of windows, floodlighting and a hundred Chinese lanterns.

Our host was not on the steps, nor at his front door, to receive his guests. No one seemed to worry: there were heaps of waiters. And there were also the 'henchmen', as my friends called them, standing alone or in pairs at vantage points, or mingling with the crowd without joining it. They did not drink, it seemed.

On the main terrace, where long tables had been set up and laden with magnificent food—*hors d'oeuvres* and sucking pigs, gleaming hams and golden turkeys—my large party had encountered another with cries of delight and were busy taking over a table for everyone. It seemed a good time to look round.

In front, terraces and formal gardens sloped down to the sea. From the lower level, with the lights behind me, I could see a jetty, a motor boat and some sort of hydroplane; there was a raft with a diving tower from which came the shrill cries of late—or early—bathers; and beyond, across the bay, the lights of East Egg whose discreet white palaces still glimmered in the twilight.

At Gatsby's house it was tango-time. It looked even larger from below, more like a hotel than the home of one man; and I wondered which was his chosen suite and whether perhaps he retired to it with champagne, caviar and a few buddies to escape the mob. Gatsby intrigued me. I refreshed my whisky at an alfresco bar and went looking for him.

Strolling along the arcades where wide windows opened into a 'renaissance' lounge, a Tiffany poolroom, a Marie Antoinette music room, I found myself sorting East Egg from West. A balding man with a girl on each arm, lamé-wrapped, swaggered out of the pool-

Right: *The house on West Egg overlooking Long Island Sound had been built in the 'period' craze; and it was said that the brewer who commissioned it offerred to pay the rents of his surrounding neighbours if they would permit their roofs to be thatched.*

DON'T go there after sunset—however determined you may be to see the real thing... There are the official tours; they would take you, in a brisk and orderly manner, round some typical Transylvanian stronghold—Bran Castle, or Hunedoara—wisely exploiting their most notorious hero. Or you may be approached one misty evening in the back streets of Budapest by a tall man with shades and a well-cut Burberry that has seen better days: he will offer you the 'true' tour. 'By full moon, naturally: we arrange it,' he adds in that charmingly accented wine-dark voice... But don't go at night.

The first glimpse of it is quite dramatic enough by day. The road, a mere cart-track, winds along a narrow gorge, following the river deeper and higher into the Carpathians. All round are snow-capped peaks like frozen waves, range upon range, till you turn the last corner, and one special mountain towers above you, splitting the sky in two: a lone volcanic peg, a canine tooth.

Close under it now, chill in its shade, you can see that one side is vertical rock. A high slender bridge, attenuated to a thread against the western light, links it to the main massif; and when you have climbed the zigzag road up this neighbouring cliff, until the birds are circling below and the river has become a tiny silver snake, it is this wooden bridge you must cross to reach Dracula's castle.

Once you are safe on the rough rocky platform, you can see this freakish outcrop is sheer on three sides, marvellously defended: no arrow, sling or culverin-shot could reach those walls; and the northern front, with its courtyard and donjonned gateway, looks out through slits, mean loopholes that give nothing away. But the great gate is open; grateful for sunlight, you enter the courtyard, an irregular hexagon no bigger than a tennis court, roughly paved and graded, with a stone well in its centre, the broad rim sliced deep by centuries of running rope. Round arches lead in under the corner towers and disappear into darkness.

There is a high wall between, and a flight of steps to the castle's main entrance, a huge iron-studded door. The broad passage beyond is pitch dark after the sunny courtyard, until dim daylight further on opens into the great hall. It is two storeys high, narrow and gloomy, illuminated by tall thin windows near the ceiling, where dusty brightness falls on the tattered drapery of cobwebs and old banners. The stone fireplace that dominates the room is carved with two rampant dragons standing on their tails; up the side columns, within each loop and peering out between the stubby claws, is a crowd of faces, the damned on Judgement Day. Crudely but energetically carved, as the guide books would say. High-backed, unfriendly chairs flank the fireplace; against the wall stands a heavy black-and-gold side-table furnished with two gilt candlesticks and an oil lamp. The walls are decorated with a show of arms: a fan of halberds, crossed broadswords, and a huge culverin over the arch that leads to the main staircase. There are wall-sconces for torches round the hall, along the side of the corridor and at the turns in the stair.

At the top, double doors open on a very different scene. Here is a fine and spacious chamber, well-proportioned but for the mean, high-set windows. The roaring fire in the grate, the handsome table spread with gold dishes, the rich sombre hangings, the crystal jug of

The castle's main entrance, a huge iron-studded door.

red wine—all these give an impression of life, even of welcome, after the ruined towers and stark, cheerless hall. Here the chairs are for sitting in—curving legs and Italian cut-velvet upholstery. An elaborate lamp and a pair of candelabra shed warm steady light on the covered serving dishes and bowls of fruit: you do not miss the sunlight now. You pour a glass of wine. You are tempted to explore.

Three doors. One opens on a library: a noble high-Gothic retreat. Carved oak bookshelves line the walls, and the round table is covered with newspapers and reference books, all of them English—the *London Directory*, Whitaker's *Almanack*, the Army, Navy and Law Lists—and all strangely comforting, as is the old red-leather chesterfield, more appropriate to a London club than a Carpathian fortress.

The next door is locked, but the third gives onto an antechamber, octagonal, windowless, coffinlike. You pass quickly through it to the large bedroom beyond. Even here the single window is high, narrow and barred. The furnishings are regal: tapestries covering the stone walls, a magnificent carved chimneypiece, a curtained four-poster bed. These apartments seem unaffected by time; but, retracing your way down to the hall, you will find other doors unlocked, and furnished rooms quite destroyed by moths, rats and neglect: rusty armour, the rotted remains of day-beds, wall-hangings; and over all, fungus, bat droppings, thick choking dust—rooms apparently untouched for hundreds of years, yet not even vandalised. And you wonder why.

Up another short winding staircase from the ground floor,

Right: *Upstairs, doors open on a more welcoming room: rich, sombre and almost comfortable. A table set with gold dishes; hot food; red wine.*

The hall is tall and gloomy, a full two storeys, with narrow windows set high, letting in shafts of light.

84

there is a door that has dropped on its hinges; that scrapes, creaks and gives way if you push hard enough. It is worth the effort: here at last huge casement windows give onto the south and west; sun streams through dusty panes; if you raise the sash and prop it open, you can look out over the glory of the Carpathians.

Standing at the casement, it is like being able to breathe again; and you realise that all this while you have been supressing your misgivings, forcing yourself to explore this forbidding place—having come so far. Admit now it was hard going: that grim hall, even those fine well-furnished rooms on the upper floor—the wine awaiting you, the blazing fire—were doom-laden and wrong, the very air thick with unanswered questions.

But this is different: bright, beautiful, spacious—and entirely deserted; that is the best part. Here, instead of glancing over your shoulder uneasily, you are free to muse and let your imagination roam. The pretty sofa by the window, the inlaid table with its painted vase of everlasting flowers, brittle to the touch, the elegant work-box—all these are signs of civilised life, the gracious touches of ladies long dead, sitting sewing and waiting for their absent warrior lords. Over centuries of summers in this sunlit forgotten room, colour, comfort and charm have been magically preserved, fixed in amber. The warmth is lulling; the dusty pink sofa with its brocade cushions invites you to rest a while in front of that view...

But be warned: you must move on. Your eyelids feel heavy as you lean back, dreaming of thin music from the spinet in the corner; but, stay any longer, and those long-dead ladies may become too real, taking shape in the spinning motes that thicken the sunbeams. You see, it is not as safe as you think, *anywhere*: the sun is already over the western peaks, and you must not linger.

Still, there is time to visit the chapel before you go; you must not miss the chapel. The only way I know is through the Count's own bedchamber. Go back to the sombre dining room—so cold despite the fire in the hearth, where the dragon-headed firedogs seem to coil and ripple in the flames: that other door is open now.

South-facing, handsome, but barely furnished, the master bedroom is unused, it seems and not one footprint on the dusty floor. The ornate fireplace is very fine; you can see the carved babies clearly now in the horizontal sunlight. It brings out the rich grain of the polished wood, spotlights the expressions of the small round faces, the gestures of the chubby hands—not gambolling but writhing, arms outstretched, mouths agape, struggling to escape those pretty birds with their tiny ears and peculiar wings.

That is the door that leads down to the chapel. As you go to open it, you catch sight of a rubbish heap sprawled in one corner of the noble bedchamber: a glittering midden. So the room *is* used... It is a mound of tarnished coins—Roman, Greek, Hungarian, Turkish: a priceless hoard; and tangled in with them are necklaces and armlets and chains of office heavily encrusted with jewels, and with grime. Why has no one taken them? you wonder, backing away as all the others have done.

Through the corner door and descending a tight, steep, spiral stair lit at intervals by loopholes, you may wish you had brought the lamp along. At the bottom it is even darker, a foul-smelling tunnel;

Right: *In this gracious drawing room with its wide view, the ladies of the castle used to sit and sew, and watch for the gleam of armour in the pass, the proud dragon standards advancing along the valley road, the return of their warrior lords.*

86

don't reach out to feel your way along, or you will raise a choking scrabble of bats; trust the semicircular patch of paler darkness and go towards it: the entrance of the ruined chapel.

Its roof is broken in several places, and the sanctuary seems to have been vandalised: the paving uprooted and heaped against the wall, the earth beneath dug into rough mounds. It is curiously shocking, this crazy wasteland, and beyond it, the cracked altar, the broken marble crucifix at its foot: more desolate than fearful, for the violence is long past. Now as you gaze round, its still sadness clings like the sweet smell of damp earth and corruption in the air. Clearly, from the fragments of coloured tile and marble, that pavement was beautiful; both altar and font finely decorated. The pure roman-esque lines are half hidden now with curtains of cobwebs, heaps of rubble; stout pillars remain, their carved pedestals and crowns peopled with faces of men and beasts. If one of the stone animals on the far plinth seems to move, it is not your imagination—just another rat. They and the bats are the only living things here; they come up out of the vaults. Those steps lead down to the family burial chamber. Yes, you must explore that too: it is time to meet your host.

Fifty coffins lie there filled with sacred, desecrated earth, and in the fiftieth lies Count Dracula himself. Go on—but you must hurry now: through the stained glass of the narrow west window the sun is very low, reaching right across to the foot of the altar and shining red on the broken cross. Make haste. I think there is still time.

Count Dracula's bedroom seems unused: a grand bed-canopy, a tall bare four poster and a heap of grimy treasure.

which, as her host explained to Catherine, had recently been modernised and made more efficient, though still housed in the old convent's vaultlike kitchen.

Lost as she well might be amongst this multiplicity of chambers, her introduction to the courtyard at the centre made it clearer to Catherine: for the whole Abbey was built in the form of a hollow square, the middle of which was surrounded by the cloisters—yes, real cloisters at last! and these to some extent compensated for the 'new wing', the fourth side, that General Tilney's father had built not long before and in the contemporary mid 18th century style—an improvement to which Catherine would infinitely have preferred the ruin it replaced: at least the cloisters flanking it remained only as picturesquely shattered columns.

When the General and his daughter took her on a tour of the grounds, Catherine was perfectly satisfied with the view from the lawn, of two purely Gothic wings; dark oak and pine woods pressed close, forming a sombre frame. She was vastly impressed by the village of hot-houses—where even pineapples grew—by the stables and shrubberies, the pretty tea-house pavilion, and particularly by the gloomy aspect of a thick grove of Scotch firs: but through this the General refused to accompany them. How strange, thought Catherine: Eleanor says this was one of her late mother's favourite walks, and yet General Tilney shuns it! She wondered: was there perhaps some guilty or dark remorse at work in his breast? Had he been cruel to her? And how indeed *had* she died?

Later, alone in her room, she recalled the moment when, during their tour of the house, the General had prevented the two girls from entering Mrs Tilney's room. Now that she added up the clues, Catherine's suspicions grew: all was not well. The General's reluctance to follow that favourite path through the firs, his hasty, almost angry intervention on the threshold of his dead wife's bedroom, his smooth deflection of any interest Catherine had evinced in the cells, or the dark spiral staircase, together with her conviction that, in spite of those she had been shown, there were as yet many apartments unaccounted for—and had he not insisted, more than once, that Catherine should not wander about the Abbey unaccompanied?—all these odd instances together suggested a possibility of such awfulness, our heroine's heart quailed at the thought. *What was he hiding?*

Her growing unease must now be judged in the context of that first night in the Abbey, until now dismissed by her as mere overheated fancy: for now the pieces began to fall into place.

The bedroom struck her at first as quite unlike that which Henry had described, being comfortable and well, albeit simply, furnished. But it was a stormy night, with the wind howling around the ancient walls; and, as she was preparing for bed, she noticed a chest very like that of which Henry had spoken. The coincidence was disturbing: she knew she could not rest until she had examined it. For some time it thwarted her efforts to open it; when at last it yielded, she searched through it and found, hidden in the farthest cranny, a roll of paper. Then—horror! Her candle was extinguished by a powerful gust, and in the darkness she heard receding footsteps, a closing door. Overcome with terror, she cowered sleepless

beneath the bedclothes while the storm raged, the bed-curtains moved, her door-lock rattled as though someone were—But, mercifully, she slept.

Morning light seemed to make nonsense of her fears; and, though she still had the manuscript to assure her she had not imagined the night's happenings, the sunlight seemed to have transformed it too—into a laundry list and a farrier's bill! Now, however, so many other sinister elements had been added, was not that secret scroll just a little *too* normal?

The secret, she feels, lies behind the doors of the dead lady's bedroom. And is she truly dead? Might she not be walled up in one of those secret cells by her heartless husband? Such things are not unknown. Steeling herself, and vowing to pluck the heart out of this mystery, our heroine sets off, treading softly, down the long gallery towards THE ROOM...

The cloisters round which the Abbey was built were a delight to Catherine—just as she had dreamed, and better still, were in elegant ruins at one end.

Overleaf: Henry Tilney had alarmed Catherine with his highly-coloured account of how she might find her room in this Gothic abbey. The reality was an amazing relief to her—but there was one mysterious similarity: the presence of a heavy black and gold chest...

Charlotte Brontë
1816-1855

Charlotte Brontë was brought up and spent most of her life at Haworth Rectory, near Bradford, Yorkshire. Her father, the Reverend Patrick Brontë was perpetual curate there and a minor poet in his own right. Charlotte and her sisters, Emily and Ann, were educated at a clergy-daughters' school, and then Charlotte and Emily went to study languages in Brussels. She worked variously as a teacher and governess, and published *Jane Eyre* in 1847 under the pseudonym 'Currer Bell'.

'Thornfield Hall' is probably based on two houses with which Charlotte was familiar. There are many similarities between Rochester's home and the home of Charlotte's friend, Ellen Nussey, 'Rydings', near Birstall. Even more closely, it resembles 'Norton Conyers', near Ripon, the property of Frederick Greenwood, whose family Charlotte occasionally visited.

Charlotte Brontë wrote only three other novels: *Shirley* (1849), *Villette* (1853) and *The Professor* (1853). In 1854, she married the Reverend A.B. Nicholls, but she died a few months after the marriage.

Chapter 8

JANE EYRE

' "*I like this day; I like that sky of steel; I like the sternness and stillness of the world under this frost. I like Thornfield, its antiquity, its retirement, its old crow-trees and thorn-trees, its gray façade, and lines of dark windows reflecting that metal welkin: and yet how long have I abhorred the very thought of it, shunned it like a great plague-house?*" '

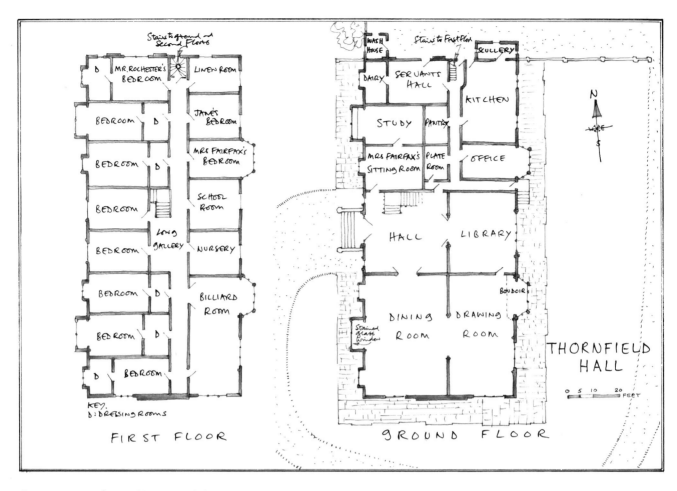

FIRST FLOOR

GROUND FLOOR

THORNFIELD HALL

0 5 10 20 FEET

I MIGHT never have discovered the house had it not been for a sudden change in the weather: my walking tour of the Yorkshire moors was suddenly halted as clouds rolled down on my late summer afternoon, and thick mist made me lose my bearings. I remembered noticing an old track across the valley, so I kept straight ahead, hoping to strike it; when I did, I stuck to it: might it not lead to some dwelling?—and clearly now I could not find my way across country to Hathersage before dark.

I was striding steadily, to keep warm, along the rough road, lost in a cold grey limbo, when iron gates loomed up suddenly out of the mist. I entered and followed an uphill drive till I came to the courtyard and steps of a great house. Only when I drew close did I realise it was in ruins; but how ruinate, I could not tell: the blackened and overgrown walls towered above me, lost in cloud, and the great hall—as I assumed it was, when I stepped across the threshold—wide open to the boiling sky, and filled with it.

Some outbuilding may still provide shelter, I thought, and made my way slowly round the outside walls; until, in a stable yard, I stumbled into a heap of rusty tackle, the remains of a carriage. All at once there came a hoarse shout: 'Who's there? Who's out there?' from a door opened in the wall somewhere ahead.

It was a rough, gypsyish woman, short and surly and with gin on her breath as she came close to peer at me. I must have looked harmless enough; and when I offered payment, she agreed, though grudgingly, to rent me shelter for the night.

Overleaf: *Thornfield Hall had long been the home of the Rochester family. In the small church near the entrance to the drive there is the tomb of a Rochester who died fighting for the Royalists in the Civil War.*

106

Her habitation seemed to be an old wash-house: low-vaulted fireplaces and rusty coppers lined one wall; sacking obscured the one small window, but candlelight revealed a ragged bed in the corner. There was an open hearth with a fire burning; she seated herself by this in the only chair—a singularly elegant piece, and, like the silver candlestick, quite at odds with its lowly setting—while I must needs make shift with a bale of straw, and was content to rest and warm myself. When I brought out my slender rations and my flask of brandy, she grew more talkative, producing two cut-glass goblets for our drams: they had been among Mr Rochester's finest: 'seen some fancy foreign wines in their day, I can tell you—and raised by some fancy county ladies—Oh, the great dinners, the house-parties there was then! The last, some dozen ladies and gentleman—more'n that, o'course, with Mrs Fairfax and the little Frenchie poppet and her governess—but *they* didn't use these fine glasses: Oh no! These were special...'

I asked her about the house, and how it came to such ruin.

'Thornfield Hall—Why, t'were one of the greatest houses for miles around. Mind you, with the Master being away so much, 'twas often weeks and months with only the housekeeper and us keeping it to rights, and that Miss Eyre, quiet as a mouse, busy teaching the child. Then we'd get word Mr Rochester was returning—sometimes with a party of gentry—and then such scrubbing and polishing, such airing of bedding and washing of they fiddly chandyliers! Oh, and such bustle with delivering of vittles, and setting out the silver, and—'

She broke off suddenly, head back, eyes up, listening. The wind was rising; I heard no other sound. I said: 'But tell me, was there a fire or some catastrophe that ended it all?'

'Aye: Fire. Fire kindled.' 'You mean, deliberately?'

'Aye: kindled in two bedrooms, the one above the other. The whole house went up, and so many precious things I'd spent my years dusting and polishing... And now poor Grace be all alone...'

'But why? Was it some act of vengeance, or madness?'

'Twere both... I dare say—wouldn't rightly know, would I?'

'And was the culprit punished?'

'In a manner o' speaking...' She nodded sagely, gazing into the embers, and would say no more on the matter. 'I'll have another drop o' that brandy, whilst you mend the fire for the night.'

'But who was it did such a terrible—?

'Hush.' Again she was listening, eyes rolled heavenwards. Clearly she was somewhat tipsy; but her next words made me wonder if she were not also a little mad: 'We'm lucky, my dear—' she said as she finished my brandy and climbed into her rats-nest of a bed—'She be quiet tonight.' 'Then you are *not* alone here?' I asked—and was answered by her snoring. I blew out the candle and settled myself as best I could, muffled in my coat on the bales of straw. The fire was cheering, but the wind moaned beyond the door, sounding through the hollows of the ruined house like a spectral organ. Listening to it—and also, I confess, for whatever the old gypsy woman had so strained to hear—I found it small wonder she should turn mad all alone in such a place...

I must have slept, for I woke with a start, shivering from cold,

E. M. Forster
1879-1855

Edward Morgan Forster was born in London. He was educated at Tonbridge School and King's College, Cambridge, with which he had a life-long connection.

Forster had a varied career as a polemicist, critic, broadcaster and Cambridge don. During the First World War, he worked for the Red Cross in Alexandria. Before and after the War, he lived in India, the setting for what is possibly his most accomplished novel, *Passage to India* (1927). Forster, in fact, thought that *Howard's End* (1910) was his best work, although he felt that the only developed character in the book was the house itself. The Wilcoxes' house was based on Forster's childhood home, "Rooksnest", which had once belonged to a family called Howard.

Forster is less well-remembered for his libretto to Benjamin Britten's opera, *Billy Budd* (1951). He was awarded the Order of Merit for his services to literature.

Chapter 9

HOWARDS END

'She remembered again that ten square miles are not ten times as wonderful as one square mile, that a thousand square miles are not practically the same as heaven. The phantom of bigness, which London encourages, was laid for ever when she paced from the hall at Howards End to its kitchen and heard the rains run this way and that where the watershed of the roof divided them.'

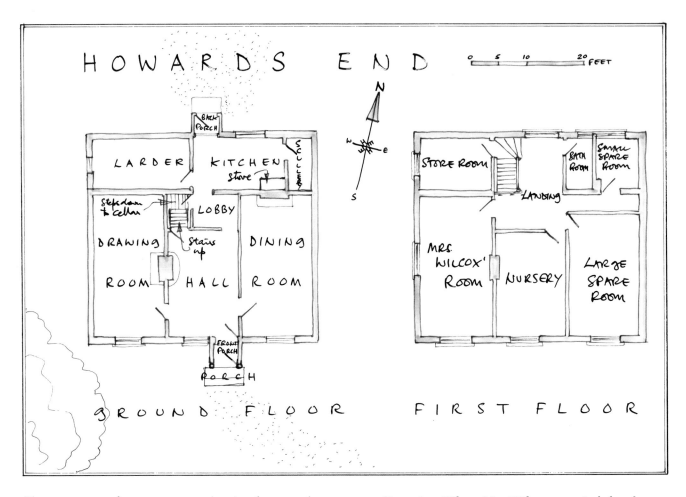

HOWARDS END

0   5   10   20 FEET

GROUND FLOOR

LARDER
KITCHEN stove
SCULLERY
BACK PORCH
Steps down to Cellar
LOBBY
DRAWING ROOM
Stairs up
HALL
DINING ROOM
FRONT PORCH
PORCH

FIRST FLOOR

STORE ROOM
LANDING
BATH ROOM
SMALL SPARE ROOM
MRS. WILCOX' ROOM
NURSERY
LARGE SPARE ROOM

THERE are some houses, even quite simple ones, that are complicated by being different things to different people. To some they represent property; to others, an outgrown childhood: too small and faded for their big, bright ambitions. But for two or three who have lived there long, or who simply sense an affinity at first sight—like falling in love—a special house can invade their blood-stream, can alter their lives. Such a house is Howards End; and for these few it becomes alive and sentient; needing love, demanding company; never dead, however empty and deserted: just waiting to be woken.

It has been empty for over a year. After Ruth Wilcox's death, her family let it and moved to London; now the tenant too has left, and the garden that Mr Wilcox had so thoroughly rationalised and set in order—felling and pruning, tearing down old outbuildings and putting up a new garage, creating purposeful areas: tennis court, croquet lawn, rockery, neat flower-beds—all this has reverted to a wild disorderly beauty of meadow-grass and briar roses, and willow-herb sprouting between the paving stones. The grape-vine that was trained against the front of the house has taken over; now, in its first flush of bright translucent leaves, it arches out from the wall and trails across the windows. The smart garage—a proud novelty, even now in 1910, for motor cars are still rare—has been sealed up by deep grass and garlanded with two years' bindweed; briars spring triumphantly from the stocks of the prim suburban roses; the remains of the border is a bright tangle, where tulips and stately irises push up through campion and convolvulus. Moreover this air of

When Mrs Wilcox married, her husband sold some of the land to improve the house. He pulled down the dairy at the back and added the kitchen quarters. The old kitchen became the hall, its great fireplace covered in.

Sitting in the porch, you can see across parkland and farms to the distant Chilterns.

neglect is strangely becoming: a 'sweet disorder in the dress' that enhances the mystery of the isolated house.

Howards End is no more than a plain brick farmhouse, some two hundred years old; its porch and kitchen quarters have been added recently; yet that mellow brick front with its nine windows draw your eyes back again and again, almost as though you vaguely recognised and are trying to place it. It is, quite simply, a house you take to; neglected, yes; but sad only because it has been deserted. The nine windows are blind with white shutters, and round at the back, where the unpruned orchard is still thick with blossom, the kitchen and store-room windows are not only barred but seem to have been covered over with makeshift screens—packing-case lids, bits of cardboard—as though to keep a secret.

Then you realise that there is movement inside the house. While you were exploring the garden, some of the shutters have been folded back, and curtains show in the downstairs windows. The front door gives way to your knock and swings open.

You are in the hall, the centre of the house. The old kitchen used to be here, before Mr Wilcox built the extension, and it still has an air of importance: the gathering place. Now a great unpacking is afoot. Behind the shutters someone has been opening tea-chests and setting out knicknacks on every surface. The curtains are at odds with the wallpaper, the pictures do not fit the shadows of others that have gone; little rows of jugs and clusters of statues stand about as though on show—and the general impression is one of a superior

Overleaf: *You are in the hall, the centre of the house. The old kitchen used to be here and it still has an air of importance; the gathering place. Now a great unpacking is afoot.*

junk-shop, but, at the same time, curiously right: these possessions seem to have come home.

Four doors open off the hall: two facing you, and others left and right to the chief reception rooms. On the left, its west window shaded greenly by the giant wych-elm that bends over the house, the drawing room has been conventionally arranged with sofas, tables and button-backed easy chairs. The curtains are too long, but have been laid neatly sideways as though kneeling. The faded William Morris paper is a sympathetic background, and the brighter rectangles where, again, pictures used to hang, now act as ornamental frames for a set of handsome majolica bowls. In the dining room opposite, a Victorian chiffonier in place of a sideboard brings a feminine, almost boudoir, touch to the plain lines. Chairs are quaintly arranged in pairs; sunlight streams in through the straggling vine and warms them, bringing the old fruit-wood to life, and checkering the bare floorboards.

The right-hand door at the back of the hall leads through a lobby to the kitchen. The other opens on a white tunnel of stairs. Suddenly you hear a drumming, a heartbeat: for a moment it seems the house really is alive—then it settles into the tread of feet, magnified by the steep tunnel. A woman appears at the head of the stairs; she descends.

She is a tall, gaunt old lady. She carries herself very straight, and wears a rusty black dress, a thin print overall and an alarming bonnet.

'Indeed, the house *is* empty,' she replies to your hasty apology; 'in a manner of speaking, that is. Ruth Wilcox, like her mother before her, was my friend. I am Miss Avery, from the farm. She is gone—she died, you know; but very soon now, I feel, someone is coming who *belongs* to Howards End. Yes, these are her possessions; only stored here, I was informed. Still, it would be sad, don't you think? not to let them out? Make them comfortable—let the sun get at them. And they look right... Come and see the rest,' she said; 'See if you think she'll like it... I haven't arranged the wardrobes upstairs, mind: I must get help from the farm lads—All this? Yes, I fixed it myself.' She beams. 'The removal men set up the bookcase, of course, but the rest—well, it was a pleasure. I come over most days for a while. I love this house: it's still so full of *her*. Strange—or maybe not: maybe it follows—but the new one, the new Mrs Wilcox, is very like her; has her way of walking, even... I can see her now, walking up the paddock or through the orchard—how she used to love it after the hay was cut: she'd carry a wisp of it about with her. Sniffing it. Trailing through the dew...

'This was her house you see; not Mr Wilcox's—Oh no! He set his mark on it, mind: "developing" it, he said. Had to sell off a lot of the land, but, give him his due, he saved the house. He's a very practical man, and believes in progress—one sort of progress, anyway: the sort that brings the cars, and the factories, and smoke and all that, nearer.'

Now you are in the 'nursery' where she proudly points out the old-fashioned bassinet cot she has set up. 'Freshly laundered,' she says, 'and the curtains too. This always was the nursery—and will be again.' From here you look out across a meadow to the parks of

Right: *The middle room on the first floor has always been the nursery. Miss Avery has unpacked and set up a bassinet, and the room is coming alive again.*

123

great houses, and beyond to ploughed farmlands melting away towards the distant escarpment of the Chilterns. 'You can still see the
corners of four counties from here,' says Miss Avery. 'True, it looks
peaceful enough; but London is spreading out towards us... And of
course Mr Wilcox always saw the good sense of improving Howards
End, making it more valuable. Now—now he plans to sell it. Yes, so
I hear. Be that as it may, I've seen two generations here, and I believe
I shall live to see another.' She shakes her head and laughs, patting
the bassinet. 'It's all ready, you see.' It is indeed; the rooms feel
freshly aired; there are towels, soap and a nosegay of wild flowers in
each.

Downstairs in the hall again she says: 'I see you're looking at
the sword—and well you may wonder why a naked sabre should be
given pride of place on the bookshelf. It's important, you see. As yet
I don't know why; but it had to be *there*... Can I see into the future?
Well, yes, my dear; but as in a glass, darkly. I'll tell you something
odd—odd in what I see: there has to be a death before there's a birth.
That's what I see. And he'll never know about his child: that's sad-
der even than a death, don't you think? But enough of my old wives'
tales. You wanted a cup of water.'

She takes you through to the cool kitchen with its blue and
white tiled floor. Now the window is clear. Looking out into the
orchard, you catch a glimpse through boughs of a slowly trailing
figure. 'Mrs Wilcox? Yes, that's her. *My* Mrs Wilcox, bless her
soul...'

*The dining room with 'Mother's
chiffonier' and the chairs from the
London house, after years in a sun-
less north room.*

Right: *The kitchen still needs to be
arranged, as Miss Avery points out;
but there is a fine view of the
orchard.*

Sir Arthur Conan Doyle
1859-1930

Conan Doyle was educated at Stonyhurst and Edinburgh
University, where he studied medicine. He practised as a
doctor, firstly in Southsea between 1882 and 1890, and
then at the Front during the Boer War. Like Dickens,
Conan Doyle campaigned for social reform. He worked
to bring about change in the Divorce Law and also took
up a number of cases of alleged wrongful imprisonment.
In 1900 and 1906, he stood, unsuccessfully, as a Con-
servative candidate for parliament in central Edinburgh.
His later life was devoted to a study of spiritualism; his
History of Spiritualism appeared in 1926.

Conan Doyle is best remembered as the creator of the
detective, Sherlock Holmes, although he wrote several
historical novels, notably *The White Company* (1891).
The Hound of the Baskervilles (1892), in fact, marks the
return of Sherlock Holmes, whom Conan Doyle had sent
to his death at Reichenbach in Switzerland in an earlier
story 'The Final Problem'.

Chapter 10

THE HOUND OF THE BASKERVILLES

'The road in front of us grew bleaker and wilder over huge russet and olive slopes, sprinkled with giant boulders. Now and then we passed a moorland cottage, walled and roofed with stone, with no creeper to break its harsh outline. Suddenly we looked down into a cup-like depression, patched with stunted oaks and firs which had been twisted and bent by the fury of years of storm. Two high, narrow towers rose over the trees. The driver pointed with his whip.

' "Baskerville Hall," said he.'

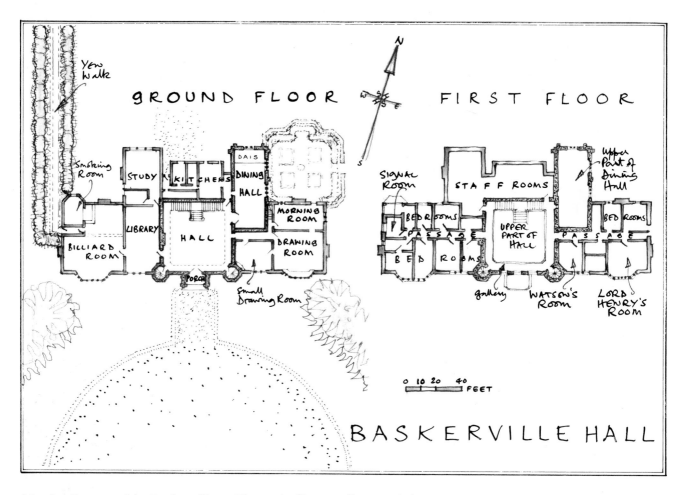

GROUND FLOOR   FIRST FLOOR

Yew Walk

Smoking Room
STUDY   KITCHENS   DINING HALL   DAIS
LIBRARY   HALL   MORNING ROOM
BILLIARD ROOM   DRAWING ROOM
PORCH
Small Drawing Room

Signal Room   STAFF ROOMS   *Upper Part of Dining Hall*
BED ROOMS   PASSAGE   UPPER PART OF HALL   BED ROOMS
BED ROOMS   PASSAGE
gallery   WATSON'S ROOM   LORD HENRY'S ROOM

0 10 20 40 FEET

BASKERVILLE HALL

THE family seat of the Baskervilles—I know it all too well—stands in a shallow wooded depression surrounded by the sombre sweep of Dartmoor, in Devonshire. Two tall watchtowers rise above the trees: with the great entrance hall and dining chamber, these constitute the original fortlike structure, some four hundred years old, and to either side, handsome wings of granite have recently been added.

One night four months ago, within the grounds of Baskerville Hall, Sir Charles Baskerville was found lying face down on the gravel path of the long yew alley. He was dead. The cause of death was found to be a heart attack; and even the extreme facial distortion—such as to make him barely recognisable to his physician Dr Mortimer—was explained as being in keeping with cardiac failure. He was greatly mourned: generous philanthropist and a good landlord and master, as well as an active politician, Sir Charles, in the few years since he returned from South Africa with a fortune, had devoted himself to the ancestral home and community where his family had dwelt for centuries; to restoring the fallen grandeur of his line and serving his county.

Two aspects of Sir Charles's sudden demise puzzled his friends. The old baronet's one eccentricity had been his superstitious horror concerning the legendary Hound of the Baskervilles, a tale going back to 1647 when the wicked Sir Hugo hunted a farm girl by night across the moors and was slaughtered by a mysterious hound twice the size of those he had set on her trail. More than two hundred

Right: The entrance hall, with a fire to welcome the travellers from London: a high, sombre apartment—and mightily impressive, no doubt, to the new baronet.

130

years later, this sane Victorian liberal seemed to live in terror of the ancient curse, and the benighted moor—yet it seems, he waited by the wicket gate onto that very moor on the night of his death. Moreover, the footprints he left were a puzzle in themselves, for they changed abruptly halfway along the yew alley. As Dr Mortimer pointed out, Sir Charles appeared to have gone on tiptoe towards the spot where he died.

It was to Mr Sherlock Holmes and Dr Watson that these fears were first voiced—fears brought to a head by a coincidence unremarked by the coroner: twenty yards from the body, Dr Mortimer had observed the footprints of a gigantic hound...

Now the new heir was expected from Canada: a nephew of Sir Charles's; but what should he be told? Must he be warned—at the risk of turning him against his ancestral home?

Sherlock Holmes agreed to meet the new young baronet. He told him the full circumstances of his uncle's death; that it seemed some threat relating to the old legend might hang over his life at Baskerville Hall; and when Sir Henry, mystified but undeterred, set off for Devon a few days later, Dr Watson was sent with him, charged most solemnly to watch over him and report back to Holmes in London.

I was well aware of all this, living as I do in one of the few

Right: *The great dining chamber where Sir Henry sits to eat surrounded by his forebears.*

houses on that part of Dartmoor; I had known old Sir Charles well. The discovery of the Canadian nephew, I admit, came as a shock to me; I travelled up to London to get a look at him—incognito, you understand—and to obtain an important item, vital to my new plan. I was nearly caught out by Holmes at one moment, but ingeniously managed to evade him. Fortunately he is detained in London by other more urgent cases: little does he suspect the urgency of this one! So I have only to contend with our dogged but simple Dr Watson, who is kept busy guarding the young baronet whilst I, all unsuspected, weave my net about him.

There is, by merest chance, an added complication which I have turned to advantage: a prisoner has escaped from Princeton gaol and is at loose on the moor. He has diverted their energies and led them up at least one blind alley with the signal-light he puts up for some accomplice. Meanwhile, his ever-present threat to the whole neighbourhood keeps the moor clear for me of casual walkers, and even the stoutest-hearted farmer does not wander abroad at nights: for the convict is none other than Selden, the Notting Hill murderer.

Then there is the Hound of the Baskervilles: another good reason for staying home o' nights. It has been heard more often of late, its mournful baying echoing round the bare rocky slopes; and some even swear they have seen it—like a great black calf, they say—wandering the hills and the Grimpen Mire, that bottomless marsh that would catch and suck down any inquisitive fool who still dared to venture out on the moors after dark...

I have met Sir Henry now, face to face. He is brash, honest and deeply filled with a sense of awe and duty, to this corner of the Old Country, to Baskerville Hall—mightily impressive in the eyes of a rough colonial—and to the forbears that surround him as he sits down to dinner on the dais of his great dining chamber.

This collection of family portraits (some of them very fine, particularly the Reynolds and a charming Kneller) span some three hundred years of Baskervilles. Many a time have I sat at that table, listening to the African reminiscences of the late-lamented Sir Charles and gazing on those faces. I would trace the odd inherited features through three or more generations, or fancifully dress them, in my mind's eye, with the wigs and hats of different periods; but to one particular portrait I always found my eyes returning: that of a fine cavalier, in a broad hat, black velvet and lace. It was the likeness of Sir Hugo himself, that notorious and colourful rogue—reckless hunter, lusty drinker, tireless womanizer. Yet none of this showed in the secret countenance; and I was drawn to that cold disciplined face: it represented a certain hardness and innate pride—even though I knew his fearful death to be no mere legend. That lace-trimmed throat had been ripped open by some nightmarish monster of the moors: nightmare or no, its teeth had been real enough. Real enough, then or now.

I am proceeding with my plan. Like all great schemes, it is simple in concept—even elegant—but complex in detail; and I could not have managed without the assistance of my trusty Spanish servant to help me tend my secret weapon, hidden away on an island in the Grimpen Mire, and safe from all who do not know the unseen paths

Right: *Baskerville Hall is surrounded by woods, but one small room on the west side looks through a clearing to the moors. From here, Sir Henry and Doctor Watson saw the strange signal light.*

Overleaf: *From one of the many Neolithic villages dotting the moor there is a distant prospect of Baskerville Hall. Sometimes I like to sit there and gaze down upon all that will soon be mine.*

through those lush green sedges. Those verdant patches afford the only colour in this magnificent wasteland, this undulating sea of grey rock, dun grass slopes and withered bracken; a sea that piles up into the frowning crests of Black Tor, Belliver and Vixen Tor. In those wastes, the only signs of man are relics of long-distant habitation in the form of stone huts, or rings that once were huts—in some places whole villages unlived in since the stone ages and unbuilt by the years in between.

From one such 'village' there is a prospect of Baskerville Hall, snug in its brown encircling woods. Sometimes I like to sit on those neolithic ruins and gaze down upon all that will soon be mine; while, below me in the hollows, and leading back among the high tors along spring-green, winding valleys, lies the mire, at once my ally and main line of defence—and it beguiles me to wonder how many lives have ended there: moor ponies, sheep, stray dogs and men, all entombed for ever in the black mud below the lush inviting sedges... This is my favourite look-out point—though in these last few days I have not visited it: I have half seen, half sensed, the presence of another watcher frequenting these slopes, hiding, perhaps, in the partial shelter of some stone hut. The escaped convict is the obvious answer; but the newspaper warnings describe him as short and thick-set—and I could almost swear I saw the silhouette of a tall thin stranger high up and black against the night sky on a distant rocky outcrop. Next moment it was gone, and I tell myself it was no more than a trick of the moonlight. Strange that I fear the murderer-at-large far less—fellow-feeling, no doubt—than this unknown presence. In fact my nerves are of steel, my determination utterly ruthless—not so unlike that hard-eyed Cavalier?

I am a welcome visitor at the Hall. Sir Henry is seemingly very occupied following on with the building works and improvements his uncle left unfinished, but I observe that, even with Watson at his side, he looks for company: Baskerville Hall, for all its new comfort and old grandeur, must seem exceedingly isolated to a social, full-blooded young man. So: today, when his guard dog was out of the way for a few hours, I sent over an invitation to Sir Henry to visit us this evening. I have good reason to believe that he will come. All is ready: I think I can promise him an eventful walk home. It will be along the lines of Sir Charles's encounter in the dark yew alley; but this time there is no question of heart failure. No: altogether far more dramatic, colourful and gripping, it will be more of a hunt, this time.

The yew alley on the west of the hall
—along which Sir Charles Basker-
ville tip-toed to his death.

ACKNOWLEDGEMENTS

To Michael Waterhouse for the biographical sections and research; Edward Arnold for permission to reprint from HOWARDS END by E. M. Forster; The Bodley Head for permission to reprint from THE BODLEY HEAD SCOTT FITZGERALD Vol. I; Penguin Books Ltd for use of their editions of NORTHANGER ABBEY, JANE EYRE and THE PICTURE OF DORIAN GRAY; Pan Books for GREAT EXPECTATIONS and THE HOUND OF THE BASKERVILLES; Arrow books for DRACULA